THE TIMES OF INDIA

A THOUGHT FOR TODAY

A Selection of Quotations from Deepak Chopra

THE TIMES OF INDIA

A THOUGHT FOR TODAY

A Selection of Quotations from Deepak Chopra

First published in 2010

by

Bennett, Coleman & Co. Ltd.

7, Bahadur Shah Zafar Marg

New Delhi-110 002

Bennett, Coleman & Co. Ltd. is grateful to Deepak Chopra Foundation (www.deepakchopra.com) for providing quotations and photographs of Deepak Chopra.

Deepak Chopra Photograph by: Jeremiah Sullivan

A Thought for Today

Happiness is yours, simply open yourself to receive it.

DEEPAK CHOPRA

1 JANUARY

A Thought for Today

If you try to get rid of fear and anger without knowing their meaning, they will grow stronger and return.

DEEPAK CHOPRA

31 DECEMBER

A Thought for Today

What creates romance is the ability to see yourself as lovable.

DEEPAK CHOPRA

2 JANUARY

A Thought for Today

If you're really spiritual, then you should be totally independent of the good and the bad opinions of the world…you should have faith in yourself.

DEEPAK CHOPRA

30 DECEMBER

A Thought for Today

My intent is to Be peace,
Think peace, Act peace.

DEEPAK CHOPRA

3 JANUARY

A Thought for Today

Happiness for a reason is just another form of misery because the reason can be taken away from us at any time.

DEEPAK CHOPRA

29 DECEMBER

A Thought for Today

You will be transformed by what you read.

DEEPAK CHOPRA

4 JANUARY

A Thought for Today

Your life can only be as free as your perception of it.

DEEPAK CHOPRA

28 DECEMBER

A Thought for Today

Wisdom has become the new criterion for our own evolution. Make the breakthrough using human creativity, imagination and intention.

DEEPAK CHOPRA

5 JANUARY

A Thought for Today

When we choose actions that bring happiness and success to others, the fruit of our Karma is happiness and success.

DEEPAK CHOPRA

27 DECEMBER

A Thought for Today

My intent is to cultivate stillness in action.

DEEPAK CHOPRA

6 JANUARY

A Thought for Today

Miracles happen every day. They bubble up from their hidden source, surround us with opportunities and disappear.

DEEPAK CHOPRA

26 DECEMBER

A Thought for Today

God leaves no footprints in the material world.

DEEPAK CHOPRA

7 JANUARY

A Thought for Today

If you're really spiritual, then you should be totally independent of the good and the bad opinions of the world, you should have faith in yourself.

DEEPAK CHOPRA

25 DECEMBER

A Thought for Today

The invisible source of all that exists is not an empty void but the womb of creation itself.

DEEPAK CHOPRA

8 JANUARY

A Thought for Today

My intent today: No judgments, no labels, no definitions, no evaluations.

DEEPAK CHOPRA

24 DECEMBER

A Thought for Today

Getting close to God through a true knowledge of self heals the fear of death, confirms the existence of the soul, and gives ultimate meaning to life.

DEEPAK CHOPRA

9 JANUARY

A Thought for Today

Nothing is more important than reconnecting with your bliss. Nothing is as rich. Nothing is more real.

DEEPAK CHOPRA

23 DECEMBER

A Thought for Today

When you seek power and control over other people, you waste energy.

DEEPAK CHOPRA

10 JANUARY

A Thought for Today

If you and I are having a single thought of violence or hatred against anyone in the world at this moment, we are contributing to the wounding of the world.

DEEPAK CHOPRA

22 DECEMBER

A Thought for Today

Life itself is intelligence riding everywhere on chemicals. We must not make the mistake of thinking the rider and the horse are the same.

DEEPAK CHOPRA

11 JANUARY

A Thought for Today

The less you open your heart to others,
the more your heart suffers.

DEEPAK CHOPRA

21 DECEMBER

A Thought for Today

When you remain open to all points of view, your dreams and desires will flow with nature's desires.

DEEPAK CHOPRA

12 JANUARY

A Thought for Today

My interest in happiness was sparked by my observation that happy people are healthier. They tend to have good relationships, and they tend to be successful.

DEEPAK CHOPRA

20 DECEMBER

A Thought for Today

You are the love that is within you.

DEEPAK CHOPRA

13 JANUARY

A Thought for Today

Bliss is a profound state of peace that comes from getting in touch with the immortal aspect of your being that is called the soul. Bliss is eternal and cannot be shaken. Happiness is usually situational.

DEEPAK CHOPRA

19 DECEMBER

A Thought for Today

My intent today: Be joyful and spread happiness.

DEEPAK CHOPRA

14 JANUARY

A Thought for Today

When we share the suffering of the world we experience compassion, which leads to love which leads to happiness.

DEEPAK CHOPRA

18 DECEMBER

A Thought for Today

Love is not a sentiment, but the truth at the heart of all creations. It can solve not only our own problems, but that of humanity.

DEEPAK CHOPRA

15 JANUARY

A Thought for Today

Love doesn't need reason. It speaks from the irrational wisdom of the heart.

DEEPAK CHOPRA

17 DECEMBER

A Thought for Today

Coincidences are not accidents but signals from the universe which can guide us toward our true destiny.

DEEPAK CHOPRA

16 JANUARY

A Thought for Today

Giving connects two people, the giver and the receiver, and this connection gives birth to a new sense of belonging.

DEEPAK CHOPRA

16 DECEMBER

A Thought for Today

A miracle is letting God
do all the work.

DEEPAK CHOPRA

17 JANUARY

A Thought for Today

If we are creating ourselves all the time, then it is never too late to begin creating the bodies we want instead of the ones we mistakenly assume we are stuck with.

DEEPAK CHOPRA

15 DECEMBER

A Thought for Today

You were created to be completely loved and completely lovable for your whole life. But you do not realize this, because underneath everything you think and feel innocence is still intact.

DEEPAK CHOPRA

18 JANUARY

A Thought for Today

To think is to practice brain chemistry.

DEEPAK CHOPRA

14 DECEMBER

A Thought for Today

The union of self and spirit is not only possible but inevitable.

DEEPAK CHOPRA

19 JANUARY

A Thought for Today

Good luck is opportunity meeting preparedness.

DEEPAK CHOPRA

13 DECEMBER

A Thought for Today

Listen to the quiet, still voice beneath all that chatter which is the genuine voice of our heart.

DEEPAK CHOPRA

20 JANUARY

A Thought for Today

The next step in mans evolution will be the survival of the wisest.

DEEPAK CHOPRA

12 DECEMBER

A Thought for Today

When you are living the truth of one reality, every secret reveals itself without effort or struggle.

DEEPAK CHOPRA

21 JANUARY

A Thought for Today

Religion is a tool to bind people together, to strengthen their unity, but like every tool, it can be mismanaged, even used in opposition to the way it should.

DEEPAK CHOPRA

11 DECEMBER

A Thought for Today

Healing is finding an inner communion with something far greater than anything in the world — it is finding your communion with God.

DEEPAK CHOPRA

22 JANUARY

A Thought for Today

Nothing brings down walls as surely as acceptance.

DEEPAK CHOPRA

10 DECEMBER

A Thought for Today

All of nature speaks the same language. We are all thinking bodies in a thinking universe.

DEEPAK CHOPRA

23 JANUARY

A Thought for Today

What keeps life fascinating is the constant creativity of the soul.

DEEPAK CHOPRA

9 DECEMBER

A Thought for Today

The impulses of energy that create our life experiences are reflected in our attitudes toward life.

DEEPAK CHOPRA

24 JANUARY

A Thought for Today

The most creative act you will ever undertake is the act of creating yourself.

DEEPAK CHOPRA

8 DECEMBER

A Thought for Today

When you live your life with an appreciation of coincidences and their meanings, you connect with the underlying field of infinite possibilities.

DEEPAK CHOPRA

25 JANUARY

A Thought for Today

This is the nature of genius, to be able to grasp the knowable even when no one else recognize that it is present.

DEEPAK CHOPRA

7 DECEMBER

A Thought for Today

There are no random events or coincidences, only the universe moving in seemingly mysterious ways to make things happen.

DEEPAK CHOPRA

26 JANUARY

A Thought for Today

The spiritual meaning of love is measured by what it can do. Love is meant to heal. Love is meant to renew. Love is meant to bring us closer to God.

DEEPAK CHOPRA

6 DECEMBER

A Thought for Today

Look at any problem anywhere, and you'll find that it has its root in a failure in some relationship or the other.

DEEPAK CHOPRA

27 JANUARY

A Thought for Today

In every failure lies the seeds of success.

DEEPAK CHOPRA

5 DECEMBER

A Thought for Today

My intent is to remind myself how lucky and grateful I am for my family.

DEEPAK CHOPRA

28 JANUARY

A Thought for Today

Be happy for no reason, like a child. If you are happy for a reason, you're in trouble, because that reason can be taken from you.

DEEPAK CHOPRA

4 DECEMBER

A Thought for Today

A basic tenet of enlightenment is humility and shedding of ego.

DEEPAK CHOPRA

29 JANUARY

A Thought for Today

*You belong in the scheme of the universe.
There's nothing to be afraid of. You are safe.*

DEEPAK CHOPRA

3 DECEMBER

A Thought for Today

Keep your attention on what is here and now.

DEEPAK CHOPRA

30 JANUARY

A Thought for Today

The soul knows everything. Be who you are and your life will transform forever.

DEEPAK CHOPRA

2 DECEMBER

A Thought for Today

Physical well-being is inseparable from emotional well-being.

DEEPAK CHOPRA

31 JANUARY

A Thought for Today

The healthiest response to life is laughter.

DEEPAK CHOPRA

1 DECEMBER

A Thought for Today

Happy people are healthy people.

DEEPAK CHOPRA

1 FEBRUARY

A Thought for Today

For nearly a hundred years, we have known that the material world is an illusion. Everything that seems solid — a rock, a tree, your body — is actually 99.999% empty space.

DEEPAK CHOPRA

30 NOVEMBER

A Thought for Today

Inner silence promotes clarity of mind; it makes us value the inner world; it trains us to go inside to the source of peace and inspiration when we are faced with problems and challenges.

DEEPAK CHOPRA

2 FEBRUARY

A Thought for Today

A psychologically healthy person can, in fact, be defined as someone whose desires actually produce happiness.

DEEPAK CHOPRA

29 NOVEMBER

A Thought for Today

My intent today: Trust.

DEEPAK CHOPRA

3 FEBRUARY

A Thought for Today

Love is like water. If it doesn't flow, it stagnates.

DEEPAK CHOPRA

28 NOVEMBER

A Thought for Today

Happiness does not depend on what you have, but on who you are.

DEEPAK CHOPRA

4 FEBRUARY

A Thought for Today

Bliss is natural to life, but once we cover it over we must search for it in others. The pain of yearning is a mask for the ecstasy of bliss.

DEEPAK CHOPRA

27 NOVEMBER

A Thought for Today

Listen to your body's wisdom, which expresses itself through signals of comfort and discomfort.

DEEPAK CHOPRA

5 FEBRUARY

A Thought for Today

My body is a projection of my consciousness.

DEEPAK CHOPRA

26 NOVEMBER

A Thought for Today

Live in the present, for it is the only moment you have.

DEEPAK CHOPRA

6 FEBRUARY

A Thought for Today

The feeler behind the feelings, the thinker of the thoughts, the animator of our bodies and minds. It is our soul.

DEEPAK CHOPRA

25 NOVEMBER

A Thought for Today

Accept what comes to you totally and completely so that you can appreciate it, learn from it, and then let it go.

DEEPAK CHOPRA

7 FEBRUARY

A Thought for Today

Getting well does not need struggle. There is no enemy within. Recovery lies only at the level of Being.

DEEPAK CHOPRA

24 NOVEMBER

A Thought for Today

Don't struggle against the infinite scheme of things; instead, be at one with it.

DEEPAK CHOPRA

8 FEBRUARY

A Thought for Today

The impulses of energy and information that create our life experiences are reflected in our attitudes towards life.

DEEPAK CHOPRA

23 NOVEMBER

A Thought for Today

Take time to be silent, to meditate, and to calm the internal dialogue.

DEEPAK CHOPRA

9 FEBRUARY

A Thought for Today

Instead of defining the soul first and asking what it does second, why not look at the need the soul fulfills.

DEEPAK CHOPRA

22 NOVEMBER

A Thought for Today

The easiest way for us to grow is to align ourselves with Dharma.

DEEPAK CHOPRA

10 FEBRUARY

A Thought for Today

I'm able to summon happiness by recalling moments of love.

DEEPAK CHOPRA

21 NOVEMBER

A Thought for Today

*Relinquish your need for external approval.
You alone are the judge of your worth.*

DEEPAK CHOPRA

11 FEBRUARY

A Thought for Today

To be authentic, you have to be everything that you are, omitting nothing. Within everyone there is light/shadow, good/evil, love/hate.

DEEPAK CHOPRA

20 NOVEMBER

A Thought for Today

Your goal is to discover infinite worth in yourself, no matter what anyone else thinks.

DEEPAK CHOPRA

12 FEBRUARY

A Thought for Today

See yourself as changing all the time. Encourage change in others. When you hear yourself uttering a fixed opinion, stop.

DEEPAK CHOPRA

19 NOVEMBER

A Thought for Today

When you find yourself reacting with anger or opposition to any person or circumstance, realize that you are struggling with the reflection of yourself.

DEEPAK CHOPRA

13 FEBRUARY

A Thought for Today

The fruit of surrender is grace. A breakthrough can lead you to the ultimate surrender. Letting go is a process and eventually comes to an end.

DEEPAK CHOPRA

18 NOVEMBER

A Thought for Today

When you relinquish anger, you heal yourself and cooperate with the flow of the universe.

DEEPAK CHOPRA

14 FEBRUARY

A Thought for Today

As you approach each day, consciously channel energy into your vision. Take any quality of the soul and convert it to your own use.

DEEPAK CHOPRA

17 NOVEMBER

A Thought for Today

*Know that the world 'out there'
reflects your reality 'in here'.*

DEEPAK CHOPRA

15 FEBRUARY

A Thought for Today

Be generous of spirit. When you give, you reveal a spiritual truth, that the flow of life never runs dry.

DEEPAK CHOPRA

16 NOVEMBER

A Thought for Today

What you most hate is what you most deny in yourself. What you most love is what you most wish for in yourself. Use the mirror of relationships to guide your evolution. The final goal is total self-knowledge.

DEEPAK CHOPRA

16 FEBRUARY

A Thought for Today

Embrace every day as a new world. For life to turn into a great victory, you have to win many small battles along the way.

DEEPAK CHOPRA

15 NOVEMBER

A Thought for Today

Happiness is the combination of the experience of peace, harmony, laughter and love.

DEEPAK CHOPRA

17 FEBRUARY

A Thought for Today

Feel the world instead of trying to understand it. Flow refuses to be analysed and the same holds true for the flow of life.

DEEPAK CHOPRA

14 NOVEMBER

A Thought for Today

Fear is the product of memory, which dwells in the past.

DEEPAK CHOPRA

18 FEBRUARY

A Thought for Today

The mystery of life is your mystery to solve. Every step of the way, you must proceed without preconceptions.

DEEPAK CHOPRA

13 NOVEMBER

A Thought for Today

Everything can be understood and forgiven, but when you judge, you cut off understanding and shut down the process of learning to love.

DEEPAK CHOPRA

19 FEBRUARY

A Thought for Today

Getting well does not need struggle. There is no enemy within. Recovery lies only at the level of Being.

DEEPAK CHOPRA

12 NOVEMBER

A Thought for Today

Remember that every person you forgive adds to your self-love.

DEEPAK CHOPRA

20 FEBRUARY

A Thought for Today

I will find my refuge in spirit. The only safe place is eternity. We are endlessly renewed in each other, therefore no one ever dies.

DEEPAK CHOPRA

11 NOVEMBER

A Thought for Today

Don't contaminate your body with toxins, either through food, drink, or toxic emotions.

DEEPAK CHOPRA

21 FEBRUARY

A Thought for Today

Love is not a mere sentiment. It is the ultimate truth of the heart of creation.

DEEPAK CHOPRA

10 NOVEMBER

A Thought for Today

Shed the burden of judgment — you will feel much lighter.

DEEPAK CHOPRA

22 FEBRUARY

A Thought for Today

I am a happy person because my life has meaning and purpose.

DEEPAK CHOPRA

9 NOVEMBER

A Thought for Today

Understand that the physical world is just a mirror of a deeper intelligence. Intelligence is the invisible organizer of all matter and energy, and since a portion of this intelligence resides in you, you share in the organizing power of the cosmos.

DEEPAK CHOPRA

23 FEBRUARY

A Thought for Today

Contemplation involves holding one thing in the mind and letting it unfold. If the process is allowed to really open up it can reach very deep.

DEEPAK CHOPRA

8 NOVEMBER

A Thought for Today

My intent today: Be love.

DEEPAK CHOPRA

24 FEBRUARY

A Thought for Today

Awareness, like water, is meant to flow easily without interruption. When awareness becomes stuck, tension is created in the body.

DEEPAK CHOPRA

7 NOVEMBER

A Thought for Today

Appreciate someone or something that you ordinarily take for granted.

DEEPAK CHOPRA

25 FEBRUARY

A Thought for Today

Violence may be innate in human nature, but so is its opposite: love.

DEEPAK CHOPRA

6 NOVEMBER

A Thought for Today

The way ahead is blocked until you find the key to the obstacle.

DEEPAK CHOPRA

26 FEBRUARY

A Thought for Today

To be blissfully happy at all times is to risk senility. One needs a little 'divine discontent' for a creative impulse.

DEEPAK CHOPRA

5 NOVEMBER

A Thought for Today

Change doesn't start on the surface.
It is generated from consciousness.

DEEPAK CHOPRA

27 FEBRUARY

A Thought for Today

Your soul carries the potential, your mind carries the intention, and your brain produces the result.

DEEPAK CHOPRA

4 NOVEMBER

A Thought for Today

We aren't here to make the world evolve. We are here to evolve as individuals and then to spread that influence.

DEEPAK CHOPRA

28 FEBRUARY

A Thought for Today

The direction of life is from duality to unity.

DEEPAK CHOPRA

3 NOVEMBER

A Thought for Today

In moments of silence, realize that you are recontacting your source of pure awareness.

DEEPAK CHOPRA

29 FEBRUARY

A Thought for Today

*In bliss they were conceived, in bliss they live,
to bliss they will return.*

DEEPAK CHOPRA

2 NOVEMBER

A Thought for Today

We alone are responsible for the change we bring into our lives.

DEEPAK CHOPRA

1 MARCH

A Thought for Today

Take charge of your health through exercise, meditation, proper diet and healthy relationships.

DEEPAK CHOPRA

1 NOVEMBER

A Thought for Today

Engagement and detachment aren't opposite — the more engaged we become, the more detached we will have to be.

DEEPAK CHOPRA

2 MARCH

A Thought for Today

Attune yourself to spirit, and it will speak to you in love. Spirit isn't a phenomenon; it is the whispered truth within a phenomenon.

DEEPAK CHOPRA

31 OCTOBER

A Thought for Today

We aren't here to be good or perfect. We are here as the antennas for signals from the future.

DEEPAK CHOPRA

3 MARCH

A Thought for Today

When you fall in love, you fall for a mirror of your own most present needs.

DEEPAK CHOPRA

30 OCTOBER

A Thought for Today

You aren't here to be as good as possible.
You are here to be as real as possible.

DEEPAK CHOPRA

4 MARCH

A Thought for Today

Uncertainty is the fertile ground of pure creativity and freedom.

DEEPAK CHOPRA

29 OCTOBER

A Thought for Today

The male principle of aggression can only be healed by the feminine principle of nurturing and love.

DEEPAK CHOPRA

5 MARCH

A Thought for Today

We must not bring one war to an end or thirty,
but the idea of war itself.

DEEPAK CHOPRA

28 OCTOBER

A Thought for Today

Everything around us is change, but it all takes place against a background that is unchanging.

DEEPAK CHOPRA

6 MARCH

A Thought for Today

Our failures are stepping-stones in the mechanics of creation, bringing us ever closer to our goals.

DEEPAK CHOPRA

27 OCTOBER

A Thought for Today

Behind mortality is the aspect of immortality.

DEEPAK CHOPRA

7 MARCH

A Thought for Today

My personal experience is that with/without transcendence, life has no beauty. To live a full life it is necessary to go beyond all boundaries.

DEEPAK CHOPRA

26 OCTOBER

A Thought for Today

The inner intelligence within you is the ultimate and supreme genius which mirrors the wisdom of the cosmos.

DEEPAK CHOPRA

8 MARCH

A Thought for Today

Pure Being: The domain of the Absolute, pure awareness before it acquires any qualities at all. The state before creation.

DEEPAK CHOPRA

25 OCTOBER

A Thought for Today

Nature thinks the way we do.

DEEPAK CHOPRA

9 MARCH

A Thought for Today

There are no extra pieces in the universe. Everyone is here because he or she has a place to fill and every piece must fit itself into the big jigsaw puzzle.

DEEPAK CHOPRA

24 OCTOBER

A Thought for Today

A mind that is truly enlightened does not think of the truth, it creates the truth.

DEEPAK CHOPRA

10 MARCH

A Thought for Today

When you are in the flow, there is a certain feeling associated with it: light, open, fresh. Being in this feeling pushes out negativity.

DEEPAK CHOPRA

23 OCTOBER

A Thought for Today

There are no accidents….there is only some purpose that we haven't yet understood.

DEEPAK CHOPRA

11 MARCH

A Thought for Today

Realize that you are on a journey to higher consciousness and embrace it. Expand your awareness through meditation and contemplation.

DEEPAK CHOPRA

22 OCTOBER

A Thought for Today

If you start believing in peace today, the world has become peaceful by one person. If someone related to you follows your example, the world has become more peaceful by two people. Gradually, a sizeable chunk of society becomes peaceful.

DEEPAK CHOPRA

12 MARCH

A Thought for Today

Love is a force as real as gravity.

DEEPAK CHOPRA

21 OCTOBER

A Thought for Today

My intent today:
Listen to my body.

DEEPAK CHOPRA

13 MARCH

A Thought for Today

Surround yourself with love and nourishment and do not allow the creation of negativity in your environment.

DEEPAK CHOPRA

20 OCTOBER

A Thought for Today

Persist, you'll find peace.

DEEPAK CHOPRA

14 MARCH

A Thought for Today

Unity consciousness is a state of enlightenment where we pierce the mask of illusion which creates separation and fragmentation.

DEEPAK CHOPRA

19 OCTOBER

A Thought for Today

When we take a decision, there are two options — grievance and miracle. Only if you let go of your grievances will you see miracles happen.

DEEPAK CHOPRA

15 MARCH

A Thought for Today

Creativity keeps the flow of life fresh and new.
It prevents inertia; it dispels habit.

DEEPAK CHOPRA

18 OCTOBER

A Thought for Today

Don't try to get rid of thoughts because trying to get rid of a thought is a thought itself.

DEEPAK CHOPRA

16 MARCH

A Thought for Today

Realize you are on a journey to higher consciousness, embrace it. Expand your awareness, through meditation, contemplation and other means.

DEEPAK CHOPRA

17 OCTOBER

A Thought for Today

Our personal goal should be to align our intentions with the evolutionary impulse of the universe.

DEEPAK CHOPRA

17 MARCH

A Thought for Today

You are living your best life, when you experience love and compassion on a daily basis, when you progressively realize worthy goals.

DEEPAK CHOPRA

16 OCTOBER

A Thought for Today

Luck is the result of your connectivity to the source of creation, stay in touch with your soul and make luck.

DEEPAK CHOPRA

18 MARCH

A Thought for Today

Misery is born of failed expectations. Minimize your expectations so that you feel less disappointed.

DEEPAK CHOPRA

15 OCTOBER

A Thought for Today

Spiritual laws work well when life is normal and the mind is stable.

DEEPAK CHOPRA

19 MARCH

A Thought for Today

Read about inspiring leaders — Jesus, Mandela, or Lincoln — and remind yourself of what successful idealism looks like.

DEEPAK CHOPRA

14 OCTOBER

A Thought for Today

A shift in consciousness is the most powerful way to create change.

DEEPAK CHOPRA

20 MARCH

A Thought for Today

The awareness of impermanence makes every moment precious, and an opportunity for giving and receiving.

DEEPAK CHOPRA

13 OCTOBER

A Thought for Today

The role of a leader is to guide a shift that is already occurring.

DEEPAK CHOPRA

21 MARCH

A Thought for Today

*The more you are open to life,
the more secure you will feel.*

DEEPAK CHOPRA

12 OCTOBER

A Thought for Today

We must be motivated by looking at ourselves.

DEEPAK CHOPRA

22 MARCH

A Thought for Today

Every time you are tempted to react in the same old way, ask if you want to be a prisoner of the past or a pioneer of the future.

DEEPAK CHOPRA

11 OCTOBER

A Thought for Today

Relaxation is the prerequisite for that inner expansion that allows a person to express the source of inspiration and joy within.

DEEPAK CHOPRA

23 MARCH

A Thought for Today

Life is dynamic, learn to go with the flow.

DEEPAK CHOPRA

10 OCTOBER

A Thought for Today

You must see human nature as a reflection of divine qualities.

DEEPAK CHOPRA

24 MARCH

A Thought for Today

Fear is the natural reaction built into the mind-body system.

DEEPAK CHOPRA

9 OCTOBER

A Thought for Today

In everything that is alive, become intimate with it, joy will be born within you, and you will drop the terrible burdens of resentment.

DEEPAK CHOPRA

25 MARCH

A Thought for Today

*Learn to deal with fear and panic everyday.
But never lose sight of the long-term goal:
finding the real self.*

DEEPAK CHOPRA

8 OCTOBER

A Thought for Today

Every person is to be treated equally,
since each of us has a soul.

DEEPAK CHOPRA

26 MARCH

A Thought for Today

Our thinking and our behaviour are always in anticipation of a response. It is therefore fear-based.

DEEPAK CHOPRA

7 OCTOBER

A Thought for Today

Tolerance of other viewpoints is freely extended.

DEEPAK CHOPRA

27 MARCH

A Thought for Today

Connect with the level of peace, silence and security lying beneath the turbulence of daily life. Meditate!

DEEPAK CHOPRA

6 OCTOBER

A Thought for Today

Key to success is inner security.

DEEPAK CHOPRA

28 MARCH

A Thought for Today

Even when you think you have your life all mapped out, things happen that shape your destiny in ways you might never have imagined.

DEEPAK CHOPRA

5 OCTOBER

A Thought for Today

Ecstasy carries you completely outside your ego boundaries. In ecstasy you know yourself as cosmic ego, unbounded in time and space.

DEEPAK CHOPRA

29 MARCH

A Thought for Today

The physical world, including our bodies, is a response of the observer. We create our bodies as we create the experience of our world.

DEEPAK CHOPRA

4 OCTOBER

A Thought for Today

Allow your mind to do whatever it wants.

DEEPAK CHOPRA

30 MARCH

A Thought for Today

Silence is the birthplace of happiness. It is where we get outbursts of inspiration, feelings of compassion, empathy and love.

DEEPAK CHOPRA

3 OCTOBER

A Thought for Today

Happiness is the combination of the experience of peace, harmony, laughter and love.

DEEPAK CHOPRA

31 MARCH

A Thought for Today

Meditation doesn't force your mind to be quiet.
It finds the 'quiet' that is already there.

DEEPAK CHOPRA

2 OCTOBER

A Thought for Today

Ask for nothing less than inspiration.

DEEPAK CHOPRA

1 APRIL

A Thought for Today

When you can live with all your opposite qualities, you will be living your total self.

DEEPAK CHOPRA

1 OCTOBER

A Thought for Today

Be honest but not self-critical.

DEEPAK CHOPRA

2 APRIL

A Thought for Today

The seeker after truth discovers that truth was seeking him all along.

DEEPAK CHOPRA

30 SEPTEMBER

A Thought for Today

When distractions pull you away from the self, sit in silence until you feel centred again.

DEEPAK CHOPRA

3 APRIL

A Thought for Today

The highest form of human intelligence is to be able to observe yourself without evaluation, to be present, to be self-aware.

DEEPAK CHOPRA

29 SEPTEMBER

A Thought for Today

You want to manipulate your life, when the best course is actually to live it.

DEEPAK CHOPRA

4 APRIL

A Thought for Today

Everything that happens now is a result of the choices you have made in the past.

DEEPAK CHOPRA

28 SEPTEMBER

A Thought for Today

Even if Karma is binding, the goal of life is freedom.

DEEPAK CHOPRA

5 APRIL

A Thought for Today

In the midst of movement and chaos, keep stillness inside you. When the mind is calm, a fascinating journey begins.

DEEPAK CHOPRA

27 SEPTEMBER

A Thought for Today

My intent today: Observe my reaction before reacting.

DEEPAK CHOPRA

6 APRIL

A Thought for Today

As long as you are at war, there can be no conflict resolution.

DEEPAK CHOPRA

26 SEPTEMBER

A Thought for Today

If you look around without self-pity, you will see that your situation is a perfect reflection of who you are.

DEEPAK CHOPRA

7 APRIL

A Thought for Today

True success is the progressive expansion of happiness. It is the ability to express spontaneous joy and share it with others.

DEEPAK CHOPRA

25 SEPTEMBER

A Thought for Today

Intentions compressed into words enfold infinite power.

DEEPAK CHOPRA

8 APRIL

A Thought for Today

People are doing the best that they can from their own level of consciousness.

DEEPAK CHOPRA

24 SEPTEMBER

A Thought for Today

It is possible to be under the sway of a spiritual law without demanding complete understanding.

DEEPAK CHOPRA

9 APRIL

A Thought for Today

I recognize my ego needs. As I continue to grow, my ego needs will continue to be there; I simply allow their importance to diminish.

DEEPAK CHOPRA

23 SEPTEMBER

A Thought for Today

The law of Karma is universal — everything is affected. This means that countless influences go into every action. The whole is moving within itself. Only our local perspective creates the illusion of isolated action tied to the personal self.

DEEPAK CHOPRA

10 APRIL

A Thought for Today

I am beneath or above no one. When I am independent of the good or bad opinion of others, I stand strong in my own divine power.

DEEPAK CHOPRA

22 SEPTEMBER

A Thought for Today

Be free in your own life, as free as you can possibly be.

DEEPAK CHOPRA

11 APRIL

A Thought for Today

Spirit is passionate; without passion no one can be truly spiritual.

DEEPAK CHOPRA

21 SEPTEMBER

A Thought for Today

Asking for love is one of the most difficult things to anyone to risk.

DEEPAK CHOPRA

12 APRIL

A Thought for Today

A single word can open your heart; a single glance can tell you who you really are. Awakening doesn't happen according to the plan.

DEEPAK CHOPRA

20 SEPTEMBER

A Thought for Today

The possibility of stepping into a higher plane is quite real for everyone. It requires no force or effort or sacrifice. It involves little more than changing our ideas about what is normal.

DEEPAK CHOPRA

13 APRIL

A Thought for Today

When your attention is in the past, you are in the past. When it is in the present moment, you are in the presence of God and God is present in you.

DEEPAK CHOPRA

19 SEPTEMBER

A Thought for Today

Success is an inner state and it is satisfying without external rewards.

DEEPAK CHOPRA

14 APRIL

A Thought for Today

Life is to know that power is in the present moment. It is to know that I am that, that you are that, and that's all there is.

DEEPAK CHOPRA

18 SEPTEMBER

A Thought for Today

Apply yourself to living around people and developing the social skills that are part of adulthood.

DEEPAK CHOPRA

15 APRIL

A Thought for Today

To have a renewed body, you must be willing to have new perceptions that give rise to new solutions.

DEEPAK CHOPRA

17 SEPTEMBER

A Thought for Today

The ultimate goal of life is complete freedom, and the law of Karma has been designed to assist by teaching us about our own tendencies and patterns.

DEEPAK CHOPRA

16 APRIL

A Thought for Today

The reality you experience is a mirror image of your expectations.

DEEPAK CHOPRA

16 SEPTEMBER

A Thought for Today

When we experience pure silence in the mind, the body becomes silent also. In that field of silence, healing is much more efficient.

DEEPAK CHOPRA

17 APRIL

A Thought for Today

See yourself as changing all of the time. Encourage change in others. When you hear yourself uttering a fixed opinion, stop.

DEEPAK CHOPRA

15 SEPTEMBER

A Thought for Today

My intent today: Harness creativity through stillness, love and imagination.

DEEPAK CHOPRA

18 APRIL

A Thought for Today

When Jesus spoke of seeing the fall of a sparrow, he was referring to dharma.

DEEPAK CHOPRA

14 SEPTEMBER

A Thought for Today

Try to grow and overcome your inner weaknesses.

DEEPAK CHOPRA

19 APRIL

A Thought for Today

In the West the closest concept to dharma is grace, the loving presence of God that keeps Humanity under divine protection.

DEEPAK CHOPRA

13 SEPTEMBER

A Thought for Today

Depressed people are marked by hopelessness.

DEEPAK CHOPRA

20 APRIL

A Thought for Today

Spiritual healing is much more than a purely physical experience or even a mental experience.

DEEPAK CHOPRA

12 SEPTEMBER

A Thought for Today

Dead ends are the result of unhappiness, generally traceable to failed expectations.

DEEPAK CHOPRA

21 APRIL

A Thought for Today

Coincidences are signals which guide us to our destiny.

DEEPAK CHOPRA

11 SEPTEMBER

A Thought for Today

Practise skills of emotional and spiritual intelligence and learn to resolve conflicts with love, compassion and understanding.

DEEPAK CHOPRA

22 APRIL

A Thought for Today

There is no substitute for the creative inspiration, knowledge, and stability that come from knowing how to contact your core of inner silence.

DEEPAK CHOPRA

10 SEPTEMBER

A Thought for Today

Revive your failed expectations or learn to live without any expectations at all.

DEEPAK CHOPRA

23 APRIL

A Thought for Today

What the world needs is healing and regeneration.

DEEPAK CHOPRA

9 SEPTEMBER

A Thought for Today

The inner intelligence within you is the ultimate and supreme genius which mirrors the wisdom of the cosmos.

DEEPAK CHOPRA

24 APRIL

A Thought for Today

Make the commitment to regularly acknowledge gratitude and relinquish all grievances from your heart.

DEEPAK CHOPRA

8 SEPTEMBER

A Thought for Today

Impulses of intelligence constantly create the body in new forms every second.

DEEPAK CHOPRA

25 APRIL

A Thought for Today

For me to solve my personal anguish over war, I must transform my consciousness until violence is no longer an option.

DEEPAK CHOPRA

7 SEPTEMBER

A Thought for Today

Life means the unfolding of the unexpected. Learn to embrace those qualities and your sense of being at a deadend will vanish.

DEEPAK CHOPRA

26 APRIL

A Thought for Today

Toxic emotions are often the most harmful accelerators of aging.

DEEPAK CHOPRA

6 SEPTEMBER

A Thought for Today

Anxiety isn't a state you must endure. It's a message from the self that something deep must be solved in a new way.

DEEPAK CHOPRA

2 JULY

A Thought for Today

End any situation that overwhelms you.

DEEPAK CHOPRA

1 JULY

DEEPAK CHOPRA

3 JULY

A Thought for Today

Foster relationships that enable you to feel worthy and good.

DEEPAK CHOPRA

30 JUNE

A Thought for Today

The way you think, the way you behave, the way you eat can influence your life by 30 to 50 years.

DEEPAK CHOPRA

4 JULY

A Thought for Today

End relationships with controlling, demanding, and critical people.

DEEPAK CHOPRA

29 JUNE

A Thought for Today

You be the change you wish to see.

DEEPAK CHOPRA

5 JULY

A Thought for Today

Find your deeper wounds and heal them.

DEEPAK CHOPRA

28 JUNE

DEEPAK CHOPRA

6 JULY

A Thought for Today

Work towards a vision of the future.

DEEPAK CHOPRA

27 JUNE

A Thought for Today

When you resist the flow of life you are actually resisting your own nature, everything that happens to us is a reflection of who we are.

DEEPAK CHOPRA

7 JULY

A Thought for Today

Face the demons of the past and no longer be a prisoner of memory.

DEEPAK CHOPRA

26 JUNE

A Thought for Today

It is important that we gain emotional freedom — to be free of resentments, grievances, guilt and jealousy.

DEEPAK CHOPRA

8 JULY

A Thought for Today

Don't try to steer the river.

DEEPAK CHOPRA

25 JUNE

A Thought for Today

True love is beyond jealousy and conflict.

DEEPAK CHOPRA

9 JULY

A Thought for Today

Stand up for yourself.

DEEPAK CHOPRA

24 JUNE

A Thought for Today

Anything that creates dependency is a potential cause for unhappiness.

DEEPAK CHOPRA

10 JULY

A Thought for Today

Fear is the response to a situation that seems to offer no better solution.

DEEPAK CHOPRA

23 JUNE

A Thought for Today

Nothing belongs to anyone.
We can only exchange energy.

DEEPAK CHOPRA

11 JULY

A Thought for Today

To view anxiety as your enemy is natural, because the state of fear is very unsettling and creates misery.

DEEPAK CHOPRA

22 JUNE

A Thought for Today

You must be in harmony with your dream before it can show up.

DEEPAK CHOPRA

12 JULY

A Thought for Today

My intent today: Deep listening with my ears, my mind, my heart and soul. Look, feel, and be.

DEEPAK CHOPRA

21 JUNE

A Thought for Today

Get real, it's now or never.

DEEPAK CHOPRA

13 JULY

A Thought for Today

The difficulty of going deeper into love is that along the way there are obstacles, resistance, fear and emotional struggles.

DEEPAK CHOPRA

20 JUNE

A Thought for Today

You cannot be happy for a reason, because that reason can be taken away from you. You must be happy without a reason.

DEEPAK CHOPRA

14 JULY

A Thought for Today

Without personal bravery, it's painful to walk away from social bonds and risk condemnation.

DEEPAK CHOPRA

19 JUNE

A Thought for Today

Celebrate every loss, for whatever you lose is unreal, and once it is gone, only the real remains.

DEEPAK CHOPRA

15 JULY

A Thought for Today

The real problem is fear of being yourself.

DEEPAK CHOPRA

18 JUNE

A Thought for Today

Become intimate with your true self and all suffering will disappear.

DEEPAK CHOPRA

16 JULY

A Thought for Today

True meditation must be 24 hours a day.

DEEPAK CHOPRA

17 JUNE

A Thought for Today

The promise of happiness lies in that mysterious zone of the self where personal reality is being created every moment.

DEEPAK CHOPRA

17 JULY

A Thought for Today

Encumbering your heart with toxic emotions prevents you from fully experiencing the magic, mystery, and joy that is available to you right now.

DEEPAK CHOPRA

16 JUNE

A Thought for Today

In your own life, de-clutter and be generous of spirit.

DEEPAK CHOPRA

18 JULY

A Thought for Today

Be committed to regularly acknowledge gratitude and relinquish all grievances from your heart.

DEEPAK CHOPRA

15 JUNE

A Thought for Today

Be giving in every sphere of your life — be it relationships, work or social activities.

DEEPAK CHOPRA

19 JULY

A Thought for Today

The pain felt because of someone's behaviour should be seen as a gift in that it teaches you self-reliance.

DEEPAK CHOPRA

14 JUNE

A Thought for Today

Be emotionally intelligent.

DEEPAK CHOPRA

20 JULY

A Thought for Today

By releasing toxic emotions you can discover the gift that this negative emotion was hiding.

DEEPAK CHOPRA

13 JUNE

A Thought for Today

Learn to resolve conflicts with love, compassion and understanding.

DEEPAK CHOPRA

21 JULY

A Thought for Today

Acknowledge all the things for which you feel grateful.

DEEPAK CHOPRA

12 JUNE

A Thought for Today

Act out of love and not anger or hatred.

DEEPAK CHOPRA

22 JULY

A Thought for Today

Transform toxic relationships into loving ones.

DEEPAK CHOPRA

11 JUNE

A Thought for Today

Plan your emotional, physical, and spiritual health.

DEEPAK CHOPRA

23 JULY

A Thought for Today

Our past conditioning influences the heart's voice.

DEEPAK CHOPRA

10 JUNE

A Thought for Today

Take charge of your health through exercise, meditation, proper diet, and healthy relationships.

DEEPAK CHOPRA

24 JULY

A Thought for Today

Cultivating your consciousness to allow for something positive is where you need to start.

DEEPAK CHOPRA

9 JUNE

A Thought for Today
If you create any open space within yourself, love will fill it.
DEEPAK CHOPRA
25 JULY

A Thought for Today

See that you are not an isolated ego-personality with boundaries in time and space.

DEEPAK CHOPRA

8 JUNE

A Thought for Today

Take time to be silent, to meditate and have a quiet internal dialogue.

DEEPAK CHOPRA

26 JULY

A Thought for Today

Don't encourage a belief that creates an imaginary barrier between you and others.

DEEPAK CHOPRA

7 JUNE

A Thought for Today

Tell yourself everyday, I am a divine being and I deserve happiness!

DEEPAK CHOPRA

27 JULY

A Thought for Today

Body and soul are products of the same absolute consciousness.

DEEPAK CHOPRA

6 JUNE

A Thought for Today

When the old, unwanted thoughts pop up, cancel them and choose, once again, happiness, peace, love abundance and unlimited joy.

DEEPAK CHOPRA

28 JULY

A Thought for Today

Leave marriage with self-respect than stay in it without self-respect.

DEEPAK CHOPRA

5 JUNE

A Thought for Today
We worry when opportunity approaches a little too closely.
DEEPAK CHOPRA
29 JULY

A Thought for Today

Men are expected to be partners in a marriage, not absolute rulers.

DEEPAK CHOPRA

4 JUNE

A Thought for Today
We hide deeper in the shadows
when fear overcomes us.
DEEPAK CHOPRA
30 JULY

A Thought for Today

You must develop what is called 'second attention', which transcends everyday events and sees with the eyes of the soul.

DEEPAK CHOPRA

3 JUNE

A Thought for Today

People who understand the true nature of reality, lose all sense of fear or concern.

DEEPAK CHOPRA

31 JULY

A Thought for Today

You are part of an unbound consciousness, a single field that gives rise to both outer and inner reality.

DEEPAK CHOPRA

2 JUNE

A Thought for Today

*Anything that upsets our plans,
takes us off the trajectory we are on,
can provide a major insight.*

DEEPAK CHOPRA

1 AUGUST

A Thought for Today

Reset your natural tendency to seek joy in life.

DEEPAK CHOPRA

1 JUNE

A Thought for Today

Spiritual growth is spontaneous.

DEEPAK CHOPRA

2 AUGUST

A Thought for Today

Find a way to counter the obstacles put up by old conditioning and mental habits.

DEEPAK CHOPRA

31 MAY

A Thought for Today

You should glean teachings from all directions, remaining open to changes in yourself.

DEEPAK CHOPRA

3 AUGUST

A Thought for Today

De-clutter and be generous of spirit. Be giving in every sphere of your life — be it relationships, work or social activities.

DEEPAK CHOPRA

30 MAY

A Thought for Today

At any given time the universe is giving you the best result possible.

DEEPAK CHOPRA

4 AUGUST

A Thought for Today

All of this life is for the sake of the self.

DEEPAK CHOPRA

29 MAY

A Thought for Today

Depression, loneliness, and insecurity are tangible experiences that can be overcome.

DEEPAK CHOPRA

5 AUGUST

A Thought for Today

Self-awareness is the key to personal growth, always.

DEEPAK CHOPRA

28 MAY

A Thought for Today

The wise thing is to seek help at the level where the problem exists.

DEEPAK CHOPRA

6 AUGUST

A Thought for Today

Every step of the path is accomplished through one thing: the steady expansion of consciousness.

DEEPAK CHOPRA

27 MAY

A Thought for Today

I think the highest forgiveness is to accept that creation is thoroughly tangled.

DEEPAK CHOPRA

7 AUGUST

A Thought for Today

Pay attention to your deepest spiritual yearnings.

DEEPAK CHOPRA

26 MAY

A Thought for Today

People need to accept that there is only one life and each of us is free to shape it through the choices we make.

DEEPAK CHOPRA

8 AUGUST

A Thought for Today

Every moment can be your teacher, for the outer world constantly and perfectly reflects the inner world.

DEEPAK CHOPRA

25 MAY

A Thought for Today

The only thing that is pure and pristine is your own awareness.

DEEPAK CHOPRA

9 AUGUST

A Thought for Today

When the pupil is ready,
the guru appears.

DEEPAK CHOPRA

24 MAY

A Thought for Today

*The more boundless your vision,
the more real you are.*

DEEPAK CHOPRA

10 AUGUST

A Thought for Today

There is no need for you to adopt an attitude of either despair or cynicism. Go to your religion. Look into things that are necessary for a complete inner life: giving, compassion and walking the path that leads to the transcendent.

DEEPAK CHOPRA

23 MAY

A Thought for Today

Your mirror doesn't reveal the truth that endures despite all hurt.

DEEPAK CHOPRA

11 AUGUST

A Thought for Today

I am the owner of my life,
no one else.

DEEPAK CHOPRA

22 MAY

A Thought for Today

You were created to love and be loved for whole life.

DEEPAK CHOPRA

12 AUGUST

A Thought for Today

Concentrate on who you are from the inside, not the outside.

DEEPAK CHOPRA

21 MAY

A Thought for Today

In our deepest nature each person is meant to be the hero or heroine of an eternal love story.

DEEPAK CHOPRA

13 AUGUST

A Thought for Today

Avoid people who are infected by prejudice.

DEEPAK CHOPRA

20 MAY

A Thought for Today

When you find true love,
you find yourself.

DEEPAK CHOPRA

14 AUGUST

A Thought for Today

What we celebrate is overshadowed by what we fear, deny, and unconsciously manifest.

DEEPAK CHOPRA

19 MAY

A Thought for Today

Negativity is born in the gap where love has been excluded.

DEEPAK CHOPRA

15 AUGUST

A Thought for Today

A momentous era is coming to a close. It has given rise to inspiring changes that will shape the next century. But as the light rises, the darkness rises to match it.

DEEPAK CHOPRA

18 MAY

A Thought for Today

People who live their own love stories do not expect others to make them feel loved.

DEEPAK CHOPRA

16 AUGUST

A Thought for Today

It's all too easy to escape your own worries by listening to someone else's.

DEEPAK CHOPRA

17 MAY

A Thought for Today

The voice of your dharma is there to guide you towards the realization of your true potential.

DEEPAK CHOPRA

17 AUGUST

A Thought for Today

Compassion is as valuable for the one who gives it as for the one who receives it.

DEEPAK CHOPRA

16 MAY

A Thought for Today

From a spiritual viewpoint you are always a creator. The tiniest situation in your life is not made 'out there' but 'in here', from the source of reality, which is awareness.

DEEPAK CHOPRA

18 AUGUST

A Thought for Today

Stop looking for the right one.
Become the right one.

DEEPAK CHOPRA

15 MAY

A Thought for Today

Curving back within myself I create the world around me.

DEEPAK CHOPRA

19 AUGUST

A Thought for Today

In the realm of spirit or God, suffering can be healed.

DEEPAK CHOPRA

14 MAY

A Thought for Today

*Transformation means radical change of form,
the way a caterpillar transforms
into a butterfly.*

DEEPAK CHOPRA

20 AUGUST

A Thought for Today

Today I am monitoring my hunger level from 1-10. 1 is famished, 10 is full, 5 is perfect. I am at 5. Where are you?

DEEPAK CHOPRA

13 MAY

A Thought for Today

Finding the hidden dimensions in yourself is the only way to fulfill your deepest hunger.

DEEPAK CHOPRA

21 AUGUST

A Thought for Today

Appreciate yourself.

DEEPAK CHOPRA

12 MAY

A Thought for Today

I deserve happiness. I deserve unconditional love. I deserve prosperity. I deserve good health. Keep telling yourself affirmative truths till you believe in them.

DEEPAK CHOPRA

22 AUGUST

A Thought for Today

Your assignment is to stop believing in your insecurity and constantly fuelling it. How to do that? Not through fantasies of wealth and success. Find something you are truly good at.

DEEPAK CHOPRA

11 MAY

A Thought for Today

Discover your own discontent, and be grateful, for without divine discontent there would be no creative force.

DEEPAK CHOPRA

23 AUGUST

A Thought for Today

Everyone's mind is different; you are entitled to your own measure of success.

DEEPAK CHOPRA

10 MAY

A Thought for Today

For acquiring anything in the physical universe, you have to relinquish your attachment to it.

DEEPAK CHOPRA

24 AUGUST

A Thought for Today

My intent today: Every action imbued with love.

DEEPAK CHOPRA

9 MAY

A Thought for Today

The need for security is based on not knowing the true self.

DEEPAK CHOPRA

25 AUGUST

A Thought for Today

Comparison never comes to an end.

DEEPAK CHOPRA

8 MAY

A Thought for Today

All problems contain the seeds of opportunity.

DEEPAK CHOPRA

26 AUGUST

A Thought for Today

Relaxation is the prerequisite for that inner expansion that allows a person to express the source of inspiration and joy within.

DEEPAK CHOPRA

7 MAY

A Thought for Today

The goal of the path is to transform your awareness from separation to unity. In unity we perceive, express, and are only love.

DEEPAK CHOPRA

27 AUGUST

A Thought for Today

There is greater value in being a free self who can bestow kindness and love from a sense of fullness rather than a sense of obligation.

DEEPAK CHOPRA

6 MAY

A Thought for Today

Spiritual awareness is the only way that healing can occur.

DEEPAK CHOPRA

28 AUGUST

A Thought for Today

In order to truly help others, we must have a strong sense of self-worth.

DEEPAK CHOPRA

5 MAY

A Thought for Today

I am the thinker and not the thought.

DEEPAK CHOPRA

29 AUGUST

A Thought for Today

Happiness is a continuation of happenings which are not resisted.

DEEPAK CHOPRA

4 MAY

A Thought for Today

Pay attention to your self outside the realm of your experiences and you'll discover that there is love.

DEEPAK CHOPRA

30 AUGUST

A Thought for Today

Life is ever-renewing; nature wants to fill in the aching hole created by death with light and vitality.

DEEPAK CHOPRA

3 MAY

A Thought for Today

If there were a spiritual payoff at the end of the trail, like a pot of gold or the key to heaven, everyone would work as hard as possible for the reward.

DEEPAK CHOPRA

31 AUGUST

A Thought for Today

Gradually, replace darkness with light.

DEEPAK CHOPRA

2 MAY

A Thought for Today

There is only one life and each of us is free to shape it through the choices we make.

DEEPAK CHOPRA

1 SEPTEMBER

A Thought for Today

Learn the difference between releasing a negative emotion and indulging in it.

DEEPAK CHOPRA

1 MAY

A Thought for Today

*Love is the beginning of the journey,
its end, and the journey itself.*

DEEPAK CHOPRA

2 SEPTEMBER

A Thought for Today

You find your path not by thinking, feeling or doing but by surrendering.

DEEPAK CHOPRA

30 APRIL

A Thought for Today

Having a single thought of violence or hatred against anyone in the world at this moment, we are contributing to the wounding of the world.

DEEPAK CHOPRA

3 SEPTEMBER

A Thought for Today

Negotiate with your feelings.

DEEPAK CHOPRA

29 APRIL

A Thought for Today
Not many people find the spiritual goal of life.
DEEPAK CHOPRA
4 SEPTEMBER

A Thought for Today

Share your grief with others, in moderation.

DEEPAK CHOPRA

28 APRIL

A Thought for Today

When you truly find love,
you find yourself.

DEEPAK CHOPRA

5 SEPTEMBER

A Thought for Today

You can free yourself from aging by reinterpreting your body and by grasping the link between belief and biology.

DEEPAK CHOPRA

27 APRIL